Turkey

BEV CLINE

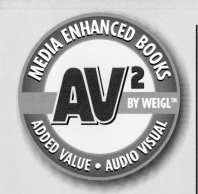

Go to **www.av2books.com**, and enter this book's unique code.

BOOK CODE

X 5 9 8 4 2 6

AV² by Weigl brings you media enhanced books that support active learning.

AV² provides enriched content that supplements and complements this book. Weigl's AV² books strive to create inspired learning and engage young minds in a total learning experience.

Your AV² Media Enhanced books come alive with...

Audio
Listen to sections of the book read aloud.

Video
Watch informative video clips.

Embedded Weblinks
Gain additional information for research.

Try This!
Complete activities and hands-on experiments.

Key Words
Study vocabulary, and complete a matching word activity.

Quizzes
Test your knowledge.

Slide Show
View images and captions, and prepare a presentation.

... and much, much more!

Published by AV² by Weigl
350 5th Avenue, 59th Floor
New York, NY 10118
Websites: www.av2books.com   www.weigl.com

Library of Congress Cataloging-in-Publication Data

Cline, Bev.
 Turkey / Bev Cline.
    pages cm. — (Exploring countries)
Includes bibliographical references and index.
 ISBN 978-1-4896-3070-4 (hard cover : alk. paper) — ISBN 978-1-4896-3071-1 (soft cover : alk. paper) — ISBN 978-1-4896-3072-8 (single user ebook)
— ISBN 978-1-4896-3073-5 (multi-user ebook)
 1. Turkey--Juvenile literature. 2. Turkey—Description and travel—Juvenile literature. I. Title.
 DR417.4.C58 2014
 956.1—dc23
                                        2014038990

Printed in the United States of America in Brainerd, Minnesota
1 2 3 4 5 6 7 8 9 0 19 18 17 16 15

012015
WEP160115

Project Coordinator Heather Kissock
Art Director Terry Paulhus

Photo Credits
Every reasonable effort has been made to trace ownership and to obtain permission to reprint copyright material. The publishers would be pleased to have any errors or omissions brought to their attention so that they may be corrected in subsequent printings.

Weigl acknowledges Getty Images as its primary image supplier for this title.

Contents

Turkey Overview

Turkey is located on the continents of Asia and Europe. It is one of the world's oldest settled areas. Since ancient times, Turkey has been a bridge between continents for trade, culture, and the arts. Some people refer to Turkey as an "open-air museum" because it has so many outdoor historical sites. The scenic country also offers mountain ranges, plains, farmland, caves, and wide stretches of sandy beaches.

Hot-air balloon tours show visitors Turkey's remarkable landscapes.

The Topkapi Palace, built in Istanbul in the 15th century, is now a museum.

Turkish outdoor markets sell spices and dried fruits.

The ancient site of Hierapolis-Pamukkale features terraces of white stone formed by hot springs.

Karagol-Sahara National Park in northeastern Turkey has evergreen forests and lakes.

Exploring Turkey

Romania

Bulgaria

Black Sea

Thrace

Greece

Aegean Sea

TU

Turkey covers a total area of 302,535 square miles (783,562 square kilometers). About 97 percent of the country is in Asia. This part is called Anatolia or Asia Minor. The rest of the country, in the southeastern tip of Europe, is called Thrace. The country extends about 1,000 miles (1,600 km) from east to west and about 400 miles (650 km) from north to south.

The northwestern part of Turkey borders Bulgaria and Greece. The eastern area is next to Georgia, Armenia, and Iran. Southeastern Turkey touches Iraq and Syria. The northern coast of Turkey is on the Black Sea. The western coast is on the Aegean Sea, and the western half of southern Turkey is on the Mediterranean Sea.

N

Turquoise Coast

Mediterranean Sea

Map Legend

- Turkey
- Land
- Water
- Lake Van
- ▲ Mount Ararat
- Turquoise Coast
- Capital City

SCALE

100 Miles

100 Kilometers

Turquoise Coast

The Turquoise Coast lies in southern Turkey between the Mediterranean Sea and the Taurus Mountains. It is also called the Turkish Riviera. The Turquoise Coast is a popular vacation area.

Russia

Georgia

Ankara

Lake Van

Ankara

Armenia

T R K E Y

Anatolia

Iran

Syria

Iraq

Cyprus

Mount Ararat

Ankara

The capital city of Turkey is Ankara. It is the country's second-largest city, after Istanbul. Ankara is located about 125 miles (200 km) south of the Black Sea. Today, it is a modern city, but a settlement has existed there for more than 3,000 years.

Lake Van

Lake Van is the largest body of water within Turkey. It is located in eastern Anatolia near the border with Iran. At its widest point, Lake Van spans more than 74 miles (120 km).

Mount Ararat

Mount Ararat in eastern Turkey is the highest peak in the country. The mountain is a volcano that has become extinct, or not likely to ever erupt again. Mount Ararat is 16,945 feet (5,165 meters) high.

LAND AND CLIMATE

ost of Turkey is mountainous. The North Anatolian Mountains stretch across the northern part of the country. The Taurus Mountains are found in the south along the Mediterranean Sea. They are part of a series of mountain ranges that extend to the east and northeast of the country.

Turkey is located in an area that is one of the most active seismic belts in the world. This means that many earthquakes occur in the region. Turkey's most severe earthquakes tend to occur in the north and east.

The Turquoise Coast has about 300 days of sunshine a year.

There are seven geographical areas in Turkey. The largest is the Central Anatolia region, which covers close to one-fourth of the land. The smallest area is the Marmara region in the northwest, which includes the city of Istanbul. It makes up less than 10 percent of the country.

The longest river entirely within Turkey is the Kizil. Starting in the mountains of north-central Anatolia, the waterway flows more than 700 miles (1,000 km) to the Black Sea. The soil in the area around the river is rich in clay. As the river flows through the region, the clay turns the water red. That is why the Kizil is sometimes called the Red River.

Other large rivers include the Euphrates and the Tigris. They flow south from eastern Turkey through Syria and Iraq before reaching the Persian Gulf. Several small rivers drain into Lake Van.

The climate varies by region. The mountain peaks along the coasts of the Mediterranean and Black Seas have snow much of the year. The mountains block moist air from reaching central inland areas of Anatolia. These areas get hot dry summers and cold dry winters. Along the Black Sea coast, summers are warm, winters are mild, and rainfall occurs in all seasons of the year. Areas near the Mediterranean have cool wet winters and hot dry summers. Eastern Anatolia has the coldest, snowiest winters of any region.

In the Central Anatolia region, near the city of Nallihan, are colorful mountains formed over time by volcanic eruptions.

1999
Year a large earthquake struck near the city of Izmit, killing more than 17,000 people.

5,178 Miles Length of the coastline of Turkey. (8,333 km)

9° Fahrenheit
Average winter temperature in eastern Anatolia. (−13° Celsius)

PLANTS AND ANIMALS

More than 10,000 **species** of plants are found in Turkey. Banana trees and date palms grow well in the warm climate of the southern coast. In the Taurus Mountains, pine, cedar, and juniper trees are plentiful. Forests of pine, oak, and beech are common in central and eastern Anatolia.

Many animals in Turkey are common in other parts of the world. Wolves, jackals, badgers, and otters are found in many regions of the country. Deer, wild goats, lynx, wildcats, and bears live in the forests.

Turkey is an important stopover for birds **migrating** between Africa, Asia, and Europe. Turkey is also a valuable habitat for bird species that are in danger of dying out. They include the white-headed duck, blue-cheeked bee-eater, spur-winged plover, and black francolin.

53 Million Acres
Amount of land covered by forests. (21 million hectares)

More Than 450
Number of bird species seen in Turkey.

THREE
Typical number of eggs the spur-winged plover lays.

200 POUNDS
Weight of the dates produced by a typical palm tree. (90 kg)

The spur-thighed tortoise lives in all parts of Turkey. It weighs about 5 pounds (2 kilograms) and eats a variety of plants.

NATURAL RESOURCES

R ich soil is a valuable resource that helps make Turkey one of the largest agricultural producers in its region. About one-third of Turkey's land is used for farming. Turkish farmers harvest more than 80 percent of the world's hazelnuts. Turkey is also a leading producer of grapes, sour cherries, apricots, and figs. Other crops include olives, walnuts, pistachios, chestnuts, raisins, cotton, and tea. Wheat is the country's largest grain crop. Turkish farmers also raise cattle, sheep, goats, and water buffalo.

Turkey is rich in **minerals**. The country mines about 60 different types. Coking coal, used to make steel, is the most plentiful. Other important minerals include boron, marble and other kinds of stone, lignite, iron, copper, zinc, lead, gypsum, and bauxite, which is used to produce aluminum.

Turkey's rivers are also a valuable natural resource. Many **hydroelectric** dams have been built on major rivers. About one-fourth of the electricity produced in Turkey comes from water power.

700 Number of international mining companies with mines in Turkey.

7TH Turkey's rank in world production of fruits and vegetables.

25% Portion of the world's yearly marble and **travertine** production that comes from Turkey.

The region around the city of Rize produces most of the tea grown in Turkey.

TOURISM

Turkey is the sixth most-popular tourist destination in the world. About 38 million people visit each year. Turkey's cities offer museums, **archaeological** sites, gardens, shops, traditional foods, and modern **architecture**. In the countryside, tourists can visit villages where traditional ways of life continue.

Istanbul, located partly in Europe and partly in Asia, is the country's most-visited city. Topkapi Palace, in the older European section, attracts more than 3 million visitors a year. Many of the gardens and low walls around the palace offer beautiful views of ferryboats crossing the Bosphorus **Strait** to the modern Asian side of the city. From the palace, visitors can walk to the Hagia Sophia Museum. It was originally a church, built in the sixth century.

Visitors to Hagia Sophia can see colorful mosaics, or artworks made with small pieces of glass or stone. They show the Virgin Mary, Jesus, and Christian saints.

Turkey has some of the most beautiful beaches in the world. Oludeniz offers calm waters and mountain scenery.

Nearby is the Sultan Ahmet Mosque, also known as the Blue Mosque because of its colorful tiles. The Grand Bazaar, one of the largest covered markets in the world, spans more than 60 streets. Its 5,000 shops sell gold jewelry, spices, carpets, and traditional clothing.

Many people visit Cappadocia in central Anatolia to see its rock sites. They were formed over millions of years by wind and rain wearing away volcanic rocks. Over time, people have carved churches, houses, and underground cities out of the rocks.

Turkey is home to two of the sites on lists of the Seven Wonders of the Ancient World. The Temple of Artemis at Ephesus, near Izmir, was built in the sixth century BC. It honors Artemis, the Greek goddess of the hunt. In the city of Bodrum are the remains of a large tomb built for King Mausolus in the fourth century BC. It is called the Mausoleum at Halicarnassus. The word *mausoleum* now refers to a tomb.

More than 12 million people travel to the city of Antalya on the Mediterranean coast every year. They visit the beaches, historic castles, and archaeological sites. Tourists also take trips into the nearby Taurus Mountains.

The cone-like formations of Cappadocia are often called "fairy chimneys."

Tourism BY THE NUMBERS

$32.3 MILLION
Turkey's tourism income in 2013.

13 Number of **UNESCO** World Heritage sites in Turkey as of 2014.

100 Feet Diameter of Hagia Sophia's painted **dome**. (30 m)

250,000 to 400,000
Number of visitors to Istanbul's Grand Bazaar every day.

More Than 200
Number of churches carved into rock in the UNESCO site at Cappadocia.

INDUSTRY

About one-fourth of the workforce in Turkey is employed in agriculture. Another quarter works in industries such as construction and manufacturing. Automobile production is growing rapidly.

Other important manufacturing industries are **textiles** and clothing, chemicals, and electronics. Turkey is also a major producer of items made of plastic. Many large international companies operate factories in Turkey. In this way, their products can easily reach the Middle East, Central Asia, Russia, and Africa by truck, train, or ship.

A number of successful global companies started their operations in Turkey. Mavi, a jeans producer, is Turkey's first international fashion brand. *Mavi* is Turkish for "blue." The Sisecam Group of Companies produces chemicals and glass. Its Pasabahce glassware is sold around the world.

16% Percentage of Turkish **exports** generated by the automobile industry.

More Than 40 Million
Number of Mavi jeans sold worldwide since the company's founding in 1991.

16th World rank of Turkey's **economy** compared to other nations.

Turkey's modern factories produce textiles for many global brands.

GOODS AND SERVICES

About half of all workers in Turkey are employed in service industries. Workers in these industries provide services to people instead of producing goods. Tourism, education, health care, and banking are service industries. The largest employer of service workers in Turkey is the government. The second-largest is the tourism industry. People in tourism work as restaurant waiters and chefs, taxi drivers, and tour guides.

Turkey exports more goods to Germany than to any other nation. It also sells many of its products to Iraq, Iran, and the United Kingdom. The countries from which Turkey **imports** the most goods are Russia, Germany, and China.

Istanbul is Turkey's major center for international air travel. The city has two airports, and construction on a third began in 2014. Istanbul is also Turkey's largest port. The second-largest port is located in Izmir.

$152 BILLION
Value of Turkish exports in 2013.

4% Percentage of Turkish exports that go to the United States.

More Than 40,000 Miles
Total length covered by all of Turkey's highways. (64,000 km)

Handcrafted Turkish carpets are highly prized around the world.

INDIGENOUS PEOPLES

P eople have lived in what is now Turkey for many thousands of years. At Gobekli Tepe in southeastern Turkey, near the city of Urfa, archaeologists have found 12,000-year-old **megaliths**. Gobekli Tepe is one of the oldest known places of worship created by humans.

1906
Year that the Hittite royal library of 10,000 clay tablets was discovered.

One of the earliest known settlements in the world is Catalhuyuk near Konya in central Turkey. People first settled at this site in about 6500 BC. The first Catalhuyuk settlement had no streets. Its houses were built back-to-back, and people entered their homes through the roofs. Many other settlements were later built at the same site.

Almost 3,000
Number of years that the ancient city of Troy existed.

18 Number of different **settlement layers** at Catalhuyuk.

People in northwestern Anatolia founded the city of Troy in about 3000 BC. In *The Iliad*, the ancient Greek poet Homer wrote about the Trojan War between this city and Greece in the 1200s BC. In later centuries, many Greek settlers came to the area.

Between 1400 and 1200 BC, the Hittites of central Anatolia created a large **empire**. They ruled for hundreds of years from their capital city of Hattusha, near present-day Ankara. By the eighth century BC, the Phrygians, believed to be from Thrace, ruled a large portion of western Anatolia. They built roads that remain visible to this day.

At the site of the ancient city of Hattusha are the remains of a sphinx gate. A sphinx is a creature with an animal body and a human head.

EARLY RULERS

Many empires wanted to control Turkey as a way to increase their trade and power. In 546 BC, the Persians under Cyrus the Great conquered Anatolia. In 334 BC, Alexander the Great marched his armies from Greece. He defeated the Persian army and seized Anatolia.

Anatolia became part of the Roman Empire in the first century BC. In 330 AD, the Roman leader Constantine I created a new capital. It was on the site of the ancient town of Byzantium. He renamed the city Constantinople, which is now Istanbul.

In 395 AD, after the death of the leader Theodosius I, the Roman Empire was split between his two sons. The eastern part was ruled from Constantinople. It became known as the Byzantine Empire. Justinian I, in power during the 500s, was one of the best-known Byzantine rulers. He collected the laws of the empire into books called the Code of Justinian. Some of these laws are still in use today.

356 BC–323 BC
Years Alexander the Great lived.

About 313 AD
Year Constantine I became the first Christian Roman leader.

MORE THAN 1,100
Number of years the Byzantine Empire lasted.

The Code of Justinian was illuminated, or decorated with colors, designs, and small pictures.

THE AGE OF EXPANSION

Over the centuries, many groups invaded parts of the Byzantine Empire. These included **nomadic** Turkish tribes. They brought Islam, the religion of Muslims, to what is now Turkey.

Beginning in the 1200s, the Ottoman Turks conquered much of the Byzantine Empire. The Ottomans were named for Osman, who was one of their sultans, or rulers. Osman and the sultans who followed him created a large empire.

Working for Suleiman I, the pirate Barbarossa conquered much of North Africa for the Ottoman Empire.

The Ottoman Empire reached the height of its military and political power under Sultan Suleiman I. When Suleiman became sultan in 1520, he was only 26 years old. Suleiman led his armies in many battles. By the middle of the 1500s, the Ottoman Empire included present-day Turkey, North Africa, the Middle East, and southeastern Europe.

Suleiman reorganized the army, government, and laws of the empire. He was known in the Ottoman Empire as Suleiman the Lawmaker. Europeans called him Suleiman the Magnificent because he supported architecture, art, and music.

In 1453, Ottoman Sultan Mehmet II captured Constantinople. This marked the end of the Byzantine Empire.

After the mid-1500s, European nations worked together to stop further Ottoman expansion. In 1571, at the Battle of Lepanto in what is now Greece, the Ottoman navy was defeated by a European fleet. An Ottoman army trying to capture Vienna, Austria, was defeated in 1683.

The Ottoman Empire later began to lose areas it had conquered. In the 19th century, Great Britain sent troops to seize control of Egypt from the Ottomans. During World War I, British and Arab forces defeated the Ottoman Empire in the Middle East. After Turkey's defeat at the end of World War I in 1918, many people in Turkey wanted a new form of government. In 1923, a Turkish general named Mustafa Kemal formed a **republic** and moved the capital to Ankara. He is called Ataturk, or "Father of the Turks."

46 Number of years that Suleiman I ruled the Ottoman Empire.

7.7 Million Square Miles Size of the Ottoman Empire in 1595. (19.9 million sq. km)

2.4 Million Square Miles Size of the Ottoman Empire in 1902. (6.2 million sq. km)

A monument to Mustafa Kemal, or Ataturk, stands in Taksim Square in Istanbul.

POPULATION

More than 81 million people live in Turkey. More than one-fourth of the population is younger than 15 years of age. In the United States, fewer than one-fifth of the people are younger than 15.

About 70 percent of people in Turkey live in **urban** areas. The rest of the population lives mostly in small towns or villages. The Istanbul area, including the city and communities around it, is home to 11.3 million people. Ankara has 4.1 million residents. Izmir, Bursa, and Adana are the three next-largest cities.

During the 1960s and 1970s, many Turks left their homeland. They moved to find work in other parts of the world. Today, about 4 million people of Turkish background live in Western Europe, and 300,000 live in North America. Others are in the Middle East and Australia.

15 Number of countries with larger populations than Turkey.

73 Years
Life expectancy for people born in Turkey, compared to almost 80 in the United States.

1.12% Yearly population growth rate as of 2014.

Istanbul is one of the ten largest cities in the world.

POLITICS AND GOVERNMENT

S ince the end of World War II in 1945, Turkey has had times of unrest and military **coups d'état**. The last coup d'état took place in 1980. It led to the country's current **constitution**, created in 1982.

The constitution provides for a president, a prime minister, and a legislature. The president is the head of state and leader of the armed forces. He or she is elected for a term of five years and can serve no more than two terms. The legislature is called the Grand National Assembly. It is made up of 550 deputies elected by the people. The prime minister, appointed by the president, is often the leader of the political party with the most deputies.

The country has 81 provinces. Each province has a governor and a locally elected council. These officials handle local issues.

1934 Year that women gained the right to vote in Turkey.

1993 Year that economist Tansu Ciller became the first woman prime minister of Turkey.

18 YEARS

Age at which Turkish citizens are allowed to vote.

The legislature meets in the Grand National Assembly of Turkey building in Ankara.

CULTURAL GROUPS

About three-fourths of people living in Turkey are of Turkish descent. Most people speak Turkish as their first language. However, there are many **dialects** spoken around the country.

A range of different cultural groups live in Turkey. The largest of these groups is the Kurds. They are 18 percent of the country's population.

In Turkey, road signs are written in Turkish, the country's official language.

The Kurds are an Iranian people. They speak Kurdish. This language is related to Persian, spoken by most people in Iran. Most Kurds are Muslim. Turkey's Kurdish people live mainly in the southeastern part of the country. Many live in the cities of Diyarbakir and Bitlis. Others are farmers and shepherds living in small villages spread around the area. Some Kurds claim that the Turkish government does not give Kurdish people equal rights. Kurdish rebels have fought against the government to try to form a separate country.

A Kurdish bride wears a red veil as part of the traditional wedding ceremony. Guests also wear special clothes.

Another cultural group is the Laz. They live along the northeast Black Sea coast. They speak Lazuri, which is related to the language spoken in the nearby country of Georgia. In the area around Trabzon, also on the Black Sea coast, are descendants of ancient Greek settlers. Some of them still speak an ancient Greek dialect.

People who speak the Arabic language live mainly around the Turkish border with Syria. In the 19th century, people fleeing from wars between Turkey and Russia came to live in Turkey. Small groups of their descendants, including Circassians from the Caucasus mountains and Tatars from the Crimea region, still live in Turkey. Armenians and Jewish people live mostly in Istanbul.

Cultural Groups BY THE NUMBERS

99.8%
Portion of the population that is Muslim.

1928 Year the Latin alphabet was introduced in Turkey, replacing an Arabic alphabet used during the Ottoman Empire.

29 Number of letters, each of which represents a single sound, in the alphabet of the Turkish language.

Muslim men traditionally worship separately from women.

ARTS AND ENTERTAINMENT

Traditions in music, dance, theater, and literature have a very important place in Turkish society. Music in Turkey includes folk, classical, military, and modern styles. Folk musicians play the saz, a long-necked string instrument similar to a lute, and the darabukka, a small drum struck with the hands. During the Ottoman Empire, military bands of handpicked soldiers called Janissaries marched with armies into battle. Their music featured drums and cymbals.

Darabukkas are played in the Middle East, North Africa, and Central Asia.

The Mevlevi Whirling Dervishes were Turkish followers of the Persian poet and teacher Rumi. Their whirling dances involved spinning on one foot. This inspired German composer Ludwig van Beethoven to write a piece of music called *Chorus of the Whirling Dervishes* in the early 19th century.

Whirling dervishes still regularly perform in Turkey.

Some of today's Turkish artists are mixing traditional music with styles from other cultures. Baris Manco was one of the first Turkish singers to combine Western rock-music instruments with Turkish folk songs. Singer Sertab Erener performs pop music in English and Turkish.

Turkish families watch a form of **shadow theater**. It is called Karagoz after a character from the traditional stories. The puppets are made of very thin camel or water buffalo hide. Light from a lamp behind the stage reflects the puppets' images onto a screen.

For centuries, Turkish writers have produced many stories and folk tales celebrating the country's history. *The Book of Dede Korkut* is a collection of stories about a nomadic tribe called the Oghuz. Children and adults read the humorous tales of Nasreddin Hoja, a wise man probably born in the 14th century.

Modern Turkish writers have achieved international success. Yashar Kemal's stories describe village life. In 1982, Orhan Pamuk published his first novel, *Cevdet Bey and His Sons*, about a large wealthy family in Istanbul. In 2006, Pamuk won the Nobel Prize for Literature.

Turkish film festivals in Istanbul and Antalya attract visitors from all over the world. Jazz, theater, dance, and opera festivals are held in many parts of the country. The Electronica Festival in the town of Cesme near Izmir brings together disk jockeys from around the world.

Orhan Pamuk is a best-selling novelist whose books have been translated into more than 60 languages.

19 Age of Turkish pop singer Atiye when she released her first album, in 2007.

12,000 Square Yards
Size of the Jurassic Land dinosaur theme park in Istanbul. (10,000 sq. m)

9TH Century that *The Book of Dede Korkut* was probably written.

SPORTS

Soccer, called football in Turkey, is one of the country's most popular sports. The first soccer games in the Ottoman Empire were played around 1875. Today, Turkey sends men's, women's, and youth teams to international competitions. The Turkish National Football Association, founded in 1923, establishes the rules for soccer and oversees professional and amateur leagues. The most popular professional teams include Fenerbahce, Galatasaray, and Besiktas. Fans in Turkey and other parts of the world follow these teams.

Arda Turan plays for the Turkish national men's soccer team.

Basketball has been played in Turkey for more than a century. There are both professional and amateur leagues. In 2012, the Turkish women's national basketball team qualified for the Olympic Games for the first time.

Turkish athletes participate in sports developed many centuries ago, including wrestling. The Kirkpinar Oil Wrestling Festival for men takes place each year near the city of Edirne in Thrace. The competition is one of the oldest sporting competitions in the world. It dates back to 1362, when most of the competitors were soldiers.

Lara Sanders of Turkey represented her country in the 2014 International Basketball Federation (FIBA) World Championship.

Another major sport in Turkey is weightlifting. It was developed during the Ottoman Empire for soldiers to build their strength. Turkish weightlifters have won medals in international competitions. Naim Suleymanoglu and Halil Mutlu each won three Olympic gold medals.

Archery is another traditional sport. The bow and arrow was an important weapon for centuries. Today, many people compete in the sport for fun. In 2013, Turkey hosted the Outdoor World Archery Championship, held near Antalya.

Every summer since 1989, the Bosphorus Cross-Continental Swimming Race is held in Istanbul. Swimmers from dozens of countries participate. Competitors swim across the Bosphorus Strait from the Asian side of Istanbul to its European side.

More than 1,600 people participated in the 2014 Bosphorus Cross-Continental Swimming Race.

1,567
Number of *Pehlivan*, or "wrestlers" in Turkish, in the Kirkpinar Oil Wrestling Festival in 2014.

1911 Year the first basketball game was played in Turkey.

1923 Year that Turkey joined the International Federation of Association Football, known as FIFA, which oversees international soccer championships.

Mapping Turkey

We use many tools to interpret maps and to understand the locations of features such as cities, states, lakes, and rivers. The map below has many tools to help interpret information on the map of Turkey.

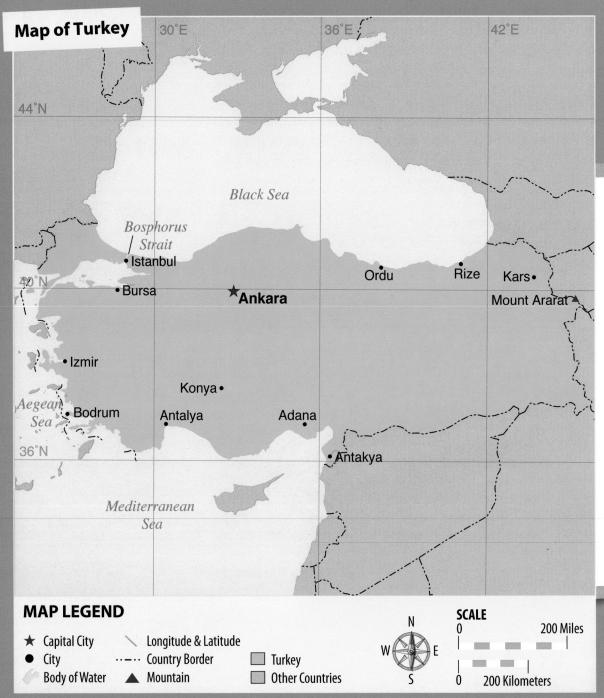

Map of Turkey

30°E 36°E 42°E

44°N

Black Sea

Bosphorus Strait
• Istanbul

40°N
• Bursa   ★ **Ankara**   Ordu   Rize   Kars •
                                                          Mount Ararat ▲

• Izmir

Konya •

Aegean Sea   Antalya   Adana
• Bodrum

36°N   • Antakya

Mediterranean Sea

MAP LEGEND

★ Capital City   ⟍ Longitude & Latitude
● City   -·-·- Country Border   ▢ Turkey
🌊 Body of Water   ▲ Mountain   ▢ Other Countries

SCALE
0 _____ 200 Miles

0 _____ 200 Kilometers

N
W   E
S

Mapping Tools

- The compass rose shows north, south, east, and west. The points in between represent northeast, northwest, southeast, and southwest.
- The map scale shows that the distances on a map represent much longer distances in real life. If you measure the distance between objects on a map, you can use the map scale to calculate the actual distance in miles or kilometers between those two points.
- The lines of latitude and longitude are long lines that appear on maps. The lines of latitude run east to west and measure how far north or south of the equator a place is located. The lines of longitude run north to south and measure how far east or west of the Prime Meridian a place is located. A location on a map can be found by using the two numbers where latitude and longitude meet. This number is called a coordinate and is written using degrees and direction. For example, the city of Ankara would be found at 40°N and 33°E on a map.

Map It!

Using the map and the appropriate tools, complete the activities below.

Locating with latitude and longitude

1. What city is located at 38°N and 32°E?
2. Which mountain is located at about 40°N and 44°E?
3. Which city is located at 36°N and 36°E?

Distances between points

4. Using the map scale and a ruler, calculate the approximate distance between Izmir and Kars.
5. Using the map scale and a ruler, calculate the approximate distance between Adana and Ankara.
6. Using the map scale and a ruler, calculate the approximate length of coastline from Ordu to Rize.

ANSWERS 1. Konya 2. Mount Ararat 3. Antakya 4. 860 miles (1,400 km) 5. 240 miles (400 km) 6. 140 miles (220 km)

Quiz Time

Test your knowledge of Turkey by answering these questions.

1 How many continents is Turkey located on?

2 What is the highest peak in Turkey?

3 What is the capital of Turkey?

4 What portion of Turkey's labor force is employed in agriculture?

5 About how many people visit Turkey each year?

6 What portion of the Turkish population is under 15 years of age?

7 What is the name of the sultan who ruled during the height of the Ottoman Empire?

8 About what percentage of Turkey's people live in urban areas?

9 Who was the person known as the Father of Turkey?

10 In what year was the Kirkpinar Oil Wrestling Festival first held?

Key Words

archaeological: related to the scientific study of human history, often by examining objects found at sites of ancient settlements

architecture: the style in which buildings are designed

constitution: a written document stating a country's basic principles and laws

coups d'état: sudden overthrows of a government, bringing a new group into power

dialects: versions of a language that are spoken or known only in certain areas or by certain groups of people

dome: a rounded roof of a building or other structure

economy: the wealth and resources of a country or area

empire: a nation or territory headed by a single ruler

exports: products that are sold to other countries

hydroelectric: related to electricity produced using the energy of moving water, such as in a river

imports: buys from other countries

life expectancy: the number of years that a person can expect to live

megaliths: large stones that are part of prehistoric monuments

migrating: moving from one region to another at different times of year

minerals: natural substances that are neither plants nor animals, such as gold, diamonds, or iron ore

nomadic: moving from place to place to find food, water, and land for their animals to feed on

republic: a form of government in which the head of state is elected

settlement layers: layers of materials deposited as each settlement is built on top of another

shadow theater: performances in which shadows of puppets are projected onto a lighted screen

species: groups of individuals with common characteristics

strait: a narrow body of water that connects two larger bodies of water

textiles: fabrics

travertine: a light-colored rock often used in buildings

UNESCO: the United Nations Educational, Scientific, and Cultural Organization, whose main goals are to promote world peace and eliminate poverty through education, science, and culture

urban: relating to a city or town

Index

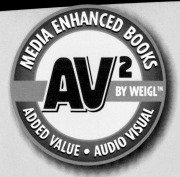

Log on to www.av2books.com

AV² by Weigl brings you media enhanced books that support active learning. Go to www.av2books.com, and enter the special code found on page 2 of this book. You will gain access to enriched and enhanced content that supplements and complements this book. Content includes video, audio, weblinks, quizzes, a slide show, and activities.

AV² Online Navigation

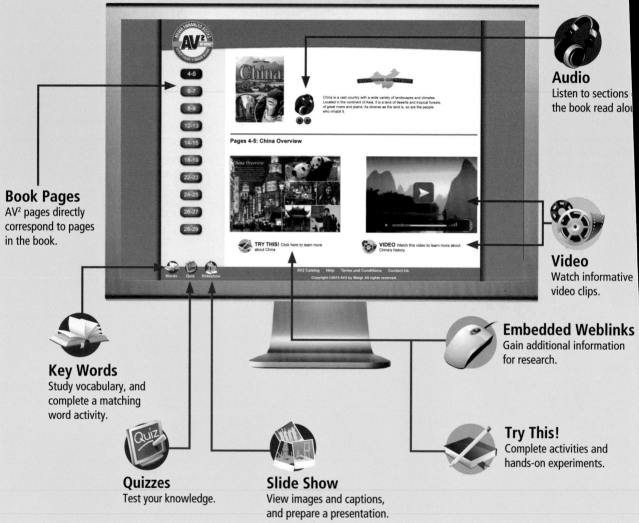

Audio
Listen to sections the book read alou

Book Pages
AV² pages directly correspond to pages in the book.

Video
Watch informative video clips.

Key Words
Study vocabulary, and complete a matching word activity.

Embedded Weblinks
Gain additional information for research.

Quizzes
Test your knowledge.

Slide Show
View images and captions, and prepare a presentation.

Try This!
Complete activities and hands-on experiments.

AV² was built to bridge the gap between print and digital. We encourage you to tell us what you like and what you want to see in the future.

Sign up to be an AV² Ambassador at www.av2books.com/ambassador.

Due to the dynamic nature of the Internet, some of the URLs and activities provided as part of AV² by Weigl may have changed or ceased to exist. AV² by Weigl accepts no responsibility for any such changes. All media enhanced books are regularly monitored to update addresses and sites in a timely manner. Contact AV² by Weigl at 1-866-649-3445 or av2books@weigl.com with any questions, comments, or feedback.